TRUE H⊥∩OS

TRUE HTUOS
SOUTH

A JOURNEY TO THE HEART OF WORKING DESPAIR

BY **ELIZABETH H. GEORGE**

RLP

Red Letter Publishing, Austin

True South: A Journey to the Heart of Working Despair
Copyright © 2016 by Elizabeth H. George
All rights reserved.

No portion of this book may be reproduced, scanned, sold,
or distributed in any printed or electronic form
without the express written permission of the author.

This book is a work of fiction. Names, characters, places,
organizations, and incidents are the products of the author's
imagination and are not intended to accurately depict any
real persons or organizations. Any resemblance of the book to
actual events, places, or persons, living or dead, is coincidental.

Book typeset by Kevin Williamson
Cover design by Kevin Williamson

Created in the United States of America

22 21 20 19 18 17 16   1 2 3 4 5

ISBN 978-0-9864371-6-8

CONTENTS

	AUTHOR'S INTRODUCTION	1
1	PLAY THE CULTURE CARD	5
2	EMBRACE NEW AGE LEADERSHIP	19
3	EMBARK ON HAPPINESS INITIATIVES	33
4	BUILD "I'M SO BUSY" STREET CRED	49
5	DAZZLE WITH DECKS AND BUZZWORDS	61
6	RE-ORG SMORGASBORD	69
7	BLOW UP THE BRAND	81
8	VOTE FOR THE FINAL CHAPTER	89
	AUTHOR'S ACKNOWLEDGEMENTS	91

ILLUSTRATIONS

1	IMPROVING THE CULTURE	9
2	DOWNWARD DOG	23
3	HAPPINESS INITIATIVES	36
4	CROSS-FUNCTIONAL PROJECT	56
5	BUZZWORDS	64
6	RE-ORG MUSICAL CHAIRS	73
7	TEAR JERKER	86
8	TRUST FALL	88

AUTHOR'S
INTRODUCTION

It seems to me that a new leadership book is published every three minutes. But this could be an understatement.

After skimming the shelves of leadership books available, I observed a disconnect between these books and the day-to-day reality of corporate life. I figured the world didn't need one more book about the leadership we'd all like to have, or could imagine only in theory.

Instead, I wondered: what if we could find insight into good leadership by openly laughing at ourselves? What if humor were used as a tool to change our perspective sometimes, even to start the most important conversations that propel our organizations forward into the future?

This book is a smart-aleck's leadership guide. It lampoons the practices we all love to hate—and exposes the warts we usually want to hide.

We all have stories to share, and I'm sure I haven't captured all of them here. Help me write the finale by sharing your most amusing corporate practices by email or on my Facebook page (see the final page of the book for more info). I'll write the final chapter(s) based on reader feedback, and new materials will appear in the next version of the book.

So, if you're ready not to take yourself too seriously, read on.

CHAPTER 1
PLAY THE CULTURE CARD

Culture eats strategy for breakfast. Or maybe it's lunch—I don't remember.

Whatever the meal, the meaning is the same: the norms, beliefs and nutty antics that comprise an organization's culture are the very things that can make or break its success. And no matter how great an executive's strategy, it's going nowhere if the culture doesn't support the direction in which he or she wants to take the organization.

If you're introducing a new strategy in your company, just know that the culture of your organization is moving in exactly the opposite direction from what you need.

You want to innovate.
Your organization wants to hibernate.

You want to drive change.
Your company wants to stay right where it is.

I say *to-MAY-to*.
You say *to-MAH-to*.

So, to help your organization leap forward, one of the most important things you must do is **change the culture.**

Your peers may have told you this is impossible, but clearly they're just not as cultured as you.

Here are **four bold leadership moves** you can make in order to transform your organization's culture:

BOLD MOVE NO. 1
MAKE EVERYONE A CHIEF

Corporations are stuffed with layers. As someone who has risen through the ranks, you know the rewards at the top of the hierarchy: a real paycheck, a parking place that isn't five miles away, and the freedom to trod on your fellow human beings with impunity. Of course, it also means an esteemed title, something like Director or Overlord. The most coveted of these titles is Chief.

Titles matter in the kingdom. Most employees duly learn that without a hefty title the only way for their ideas to get any attention is if they are (A) repeated by someone of higher rank, who takes the credit, or (2) presented by an outside consultant, who was brought in to say the exact same thing for more money than said employee made last year.

Oddly, this causes some resentment.

As a senior leader, this is your big opportunity. You have to get loud and take some bold action. Never mind that the will of your people has been bent more crooked than Quasimodo's spine; they've got ideas that need mining, ideas that might finally give you the edge over your competition. If giving people fancy titles lets us drill, then we're gonna *drill, baby, drill!*

Action Plan

In partnership with the Chief Human Resources Officer and the Chief Innovation Officer, roll out a new title structure that enables every employee to be a Chief of something. Include the Chief Marketing Officer in these discussions, since you'll need the marketing team to design business cards with enough space for the new titles—titles like Chief Meal Planner for the Company Café, Chief of Ineffective Wellness Programs, and Chief Resolver of Tweeter Complaints.

BOLD MOVE NO. 2
ESTABLISH YOUR CORPORATE VALUES

The foundation for a strong culture begins with company values. Core values will bring employees together, eliminate the need for rules and regulations, and eradicate world hunger. Values exist alongside the company's vision and mission statements, brand promise, corporate social responsibility program, *blah blah blah*—for most people it all kind of runs together.

Values and mission statements give employees a sense of purpose and lift them up from their day-to-day drudgery. It's these corporate platitudes that show them how their job selling paper clips transforms the world. "That's not just a paper clip," you proclaim from the podium, the gleaming silver metal held high in the air. "This humble device is a means of attaining synergies by combining disparate ideas which, together, have the power to change hearts and minds." *And the crowd goes wild.*

No need to waste time or energy trying to be "original" with your values. No matter how much you pay the consultants or how many surveys you collect, you're destined to end up with values that sound like everyone else's. So keep it simple and **pick the words you like saying the most:**

Integrity—because your honesty and ethics don't matter until you make a big display of them (fake it 'til you make it, right?)

Customer Focus—well, you do care about them, don't you? *DON'T YOU?* Of course you do.

Excellence—if you don't say you value excellence, people will assume you value mediocrity

Teamwork—suitable substitutes include *partnership*, *collaboration*, *co-creation*, or *synergy-ization*

Something to do with *respect for other people*

The planet. Don't forget the planet.

But you're not done once you introduce the values. After the initial excitement from the communications campaign has waned, employees will begin to ask if the company is serious about living its values. They will wonder aloud why—for example—Ass-Kicking Andy is still in a senior position.

This is when you lead by example. Show your people the powerful art of delegation by telling your HR leader to find these outliers a role "managing special projects."

Action Plan

Save yourself the money and hassle and lift a set of core values from any other company on the planet. Ask your graphic design team to create a fresh visual for the values, then pass out T-shirts and mugs to the hungry masses. Remember to lead by example, this time in terms of accountability; if anyone violates the new cultural standards, publicly throw the HR team under the bus.

BOLD MOVE NO. 3
SHARE COMPANY STORIES

Storytelling is your friend. The most effective way to demonstrate the success of your cultural initiatives is to share anecdotes and examples of how the organizational culture is transforming under your leadership. By sharing high-emotion stories with the right panache, you can eliminate the need for any real evidence or data, saving the company time and money.

The best news of all? Your stories don't have to be limited to the ones you actually know. A story's a story, and really you're just trying to make your point, so feel free to retrograde, fabricate, and custom-fit stories for your purpose. For example:

- "Bill in the mailroom demonstrated our value of Teamwork this week when he invited his colleagues in Audit to co-create a new interoffice mail process and told them to collect their own damn packages."

- "The Accounting team took on my challenge to correct their risk-averse mindset. As a result, they're only going to track revenues and not expenses. That's the spirit!"

- "Miranda is embracing our culture of health and wellness. Please congratulate her on the inspiring 25-pound weight loss. Note that this achievement bears no connection to the stomach virus that recently swept through the customer service department."

Action Plan

Send your communications team out to collect employee success stories. Claim success for your cultural initiatives by custom-fitting the stories to meet your objectives. Any employee success story from the last five years is eligible; if the story comes from senior management, anything from the Big Bang forward is fair game.

BOLD MOVE NO. 4
EMPOWER THE PEOPLE

One corporate culture effort that never, ever goes out of style is Empowerment. *Empowerment* is the process of enabling employees to think, take action, and make decisions on their own. Customers sometimes notice this, but mostly, it puts employees on the fast track to self-actualization. After all, according to Maslow's hierarchy, it's just five easy steps to beatific!

But, as a leader, empowerment presents you with a conundrum. Like other successful leaders, you have probably spent years slugging it out in the trenches, quietly back-stabbing colleagues and taking credit for work you didn't do—all in order to *gain* power.

Now some 25-year-old management consultant is advising you to *share* power. *Where's the justice in that?* You've worked hard, right? You had to do a lot of stabbing to get where you are!

No matter—it is what it is. And you need to be the bigger man or woman and begin instructing your company leaders to start empowering their teams. Some examples of low-hanging empowerment fruit:

- Going forward, let call center workers go to the bathroom when they need to. This will also save you the effort of signing their bathroom slips and calling ahead to the security guards.

- Employees should be encouraged to submit suggestions for improving operations. They should also be empowered to support their ideas with a comprehensive statistical analysis, 100 signatures of support, and a rehearsed presentation. This will enable them to deliver their idea with impact to the people who (definitely) want to hear it.

ACTION PLAN

Talk about empowerment with passion, and don't fake it—given your iron grip over every aspect of their work lives, you know how it feels to be empowered. Let them share in that feeling—a little bit.

You know . . . maybe.

2 CHAPTER

EMBRACE NEW AGE LEADERSHIP

Leadership theories are one thing you can expect to change, so you will need to rely on a gaggle of gurus for guidance in this subject.

It's important to stay current on these trends because research shows that employees leave leaders, not companies. According to available evidence, most people dislike and distrust their leaders and have one foot out the door at any given moment. So if you want to keep your employee retention above 15%, you're advised to focus on improving your leadership skills—and those of the other big animals in your company zoo.

Based on a meta-analysis of the current best-selling leadership books, **six traits have been identified as essential** for successful executive leadership. In recent years, when up has become west and east has become down, they've shifted a bit towards the right.

Or maybe the left.
I suppose it depends where you're standing.

Regardless—below is a chart showing the six leadership behaviors that have fallen out of favor, shown beside the corresponding behaviors for leaders in the modern age.

If you recognize that you and your leaders are working from the left side of the spectrum, relax. There are plenty of resources to assist you in the transition.

DINOSAUR	NEW AGE LEADER
Sits at Head of Table	Leads Meetings in Downward Dog
Professional	Confessional
Exhibits Emotional Intelligence	Cries Crocodile Tears
Pays Taxes	Organizes Inversions
Commands and Controls	Dials It In From the Burgundy Region
Works Out to Unwind	Smokes Weed in Boulder

Leadership Resources

LEADERSHIP YOGIS
These individuals have pulled from their bottomless experiences as hairstylists, electricians, high school football coaches, and ex-convicts to write bestselling books on leadership. For an additional fee, these thought leaders can conduct past-life regression therapy with each of your team members and find out which were Indian chiefs or high priestesses in a previous lifetime.

TEAM RETREATS
These meetings normally last a couple of days. They're designed to build trust—after all, it takes considerable restraint not to murder your fellow employees when you're forced to spend 48 hours straight with them.

Retreat organizers can choose from a variety of themed activities based on popular TV shows like *Naked and Afraid*, *Fear Factor*, or *Hell's Kitchen*. Drawing from these sources often brings some helpful revelations; for example, note that people usually fear Gordon Ramsey hurling insults and f-bombs more than they fear eating a live scorpion—which should prove that verbal abuse is often the best way to go.

(But bring the scorpions, too. You need a Plan B.)

360° FEEDBACK

These rounded feedback tools have been around for a long time. Their intent is to gather performance feedback from an individual's leader, peers, and direct reports. As the boss, you are entitled to 450-degree feedback, which also includes the valuable perspectives of cronies. This should soften the blow from your direct reports, who have been waiting for this moment for a long, *long* time.

"It is better to be feared than loved if you cannot be both."

— *Niccolo Macchiavelli*

Fake It 'Til You Make It

We've made a big fuss about the need for **greater authenticity in corporate leadership.** Authenticity is about being real, about speaking honestly and not being afraid to show vulnerability. Authenticity is what people crave in their relationships, and employees increasingly demand it of their leaders.

Contrary to the current wave of thinking, we advise you **not** to fall into the authenticity trap heralded by the new wave of thinking. While leadership theories are always changing, human nature remains the same . . . and human nature taught us there's always *someone* out to get you.

For the last few years, a team of social scientists has been sequestered in a musty lab conducting research on what makes people believe that another human being might be authentic, so that we might all have some answers. Unfortunately, they've spent the entirety of that time in philosophical deadlock because, in their probing and prodding on authenticity, they've been forced to endlessly scrutinize one another. Worse yet, some have lost the sense that they knew themselves to begin with.

As you can see, it's dangerous to be authentic. Starting in a couple pages, I've outlined **five easy-to-implement techniques for faking authenticity** to maintain complete power and control. No one, except you and your handlers, will ever know the difference.

TECHNIQUE NO. 1
DIG DEEP FOR EXAMPLES OF HUMILITY
Employees, customers, and partners alike will take pleasure in seeing that you are a man or woman of the people, someone who faces the same challenges as everyone else. They will smile warmly at stories of your parenting challenges, laugh at the trials and tribulations of training a new puppy, and beam with pride as you describe the first time you pulled your new yacht into its slip. "He's a real guy, too!" they'll exclaim with admiration.

TECHNIQUE NO. 2
SHARE PERSONAL PHOTOS
Photos of your children and pets are guaranteed to evoke a collective "awww" from any audience. Other photo ops include the executive taking out the garbage, the executive in a moment of reflection, or the executive arguing with neighbors about where her new swimming pool is going.

TECHNIQUE NO. 3
GET CREATIVE WITH VOLUNTEER WORK
Nothing is more inspiring than stories of executives "giving back." There are plenty of ways to give to the community, like serving a meal at a shelter, delivering Christmas gifts to an angel tree family, or donating 100 copies of your new autobiography to a school in Africa. All that matters is that it's in English, right?

TECHNIQUE NO. 4
STRETCH YOUR PERSONAL STORY
Now that you're a big shot, people will want to understand the forces in your life that have shaped you. Be ready to provide responses to journalists that will show the public the challenges you have endured and what you are made of.

Following are a sample question and answer—

Interviewer
Can you share a few childhood events that
have shaped you most as a leader?

You
I grew up in a small town running through fields and peeling the lights off fireflies. As the child of two doctors, I always had a fascination with the human body and its workings that propelled me to amass the finest collection of Farrah Fawcett posters in the region—the one of her in the red bathing suit is still a classic.

As an avid learner, I have a natural curiosity that spills into my interviews of job candidates. I want to know how they think. One of my favorite questions: would they rather eat a stick of butter or a cup of mayonnaise—and *why?* My leadership style is based on a deep respect for Chinese philosophy and I try to go with the flow most days. That's made me quite the fine surfer I am today.

TECHNIQUE NO. 5
TAKE A CUE FROM EMOJIS

Building a connection with any audience requires you to display emotions appropriate for your message. These are tried-and-true facial expressions that will instantly demonstrate sincerity for a variety of messages. Be sure to practice in the mirror so you can put them on at a moment's notice.

See below for guidance:

 The competition took us by surprise!

 I sincerely regret the recent layoffs.

 *The new girl in Accounting is hot!*

CHAPTER 3
EMBARK ON HAPPINESS INITIATIVES

Knowing how to motivate your employees, and thus get the most out of them, is essential to running a successful company.

The larger the company, the more challenging this can be, and the more time and resources you'll need to crack the employee engagement code.

Like any good leader, you have probably spent millions on employee engagement consultants. So I'm going to ask you to sit down and take a deep breath for this next piece, because I need to share some grave news.

In the last couple of years, **engagement has made way for something deeper and more profound:** *employee happiness.* That's right—I said it. If you want to attract and retain the best talent, you need to figure out what even the greatest philosophers struggled to figure out.

I know what you're thinking: *I didn't sign up for this.*

What happened to the good old days, when it was good enough for employees to just be satisfied?

Don't worry: there's a huge volume of research available to help you create a fulfilled and painfully happy workforce. Best of all, none of these methods requires you to share that fat bonus of yours.

The Workspace

One very important factor in employee happiness is their physical workspace. Employees yearn for workspaces that are tailored to the work they do, that accommodate their introverted or extroverted work styles, and that provide them with the necessary tools for success, like access to a copy room where they can photocopy their body parts on slow days.

Take inspiration from some of America's best places to work and create innovative workspaces like:

Meditation Medinas—complete with shamanic drums to help employees connect with their spirit animals.

Community Lounges—where employees can wear their pajamas and watch old movies on TCM (or AMC, if you're too cheap for premium cable).

Unisex Lactation Rooms—because, at some point, women are going to demand that men at least *try* this breast-feeding business.

Game Room—a couple of PCs running *Minecraft* should do the trick. *Minecraft* is a good choice because it's a game where players basically have to work nonstop to survive, which is a theme employees will recognize.

Multi-Purpose Spaces—if you're short on space, consider combining two or more of the above ideas into, for instance, shamanic movie spaces or a virtual lactation room.

COLLABORATIVE SPACE

Creating the right type of space can also encourage collaboration, which is important since employees, on their own, tend to focus on their own individual tasks and assume that other departments' work is a complete waste of time and resources. Back in the day, some whiz kid got the idea that corporations could fix this silo problem by building coffee shops inside their own walls. These gathering places would build a sense of community and encourage innovation through serene and friendly interactions. That was the *idea*.

Save yourself some valuable real estate by buying every employee a Starbucks gift card instead. Let someone else worry about making sweet potato pie cappuccinos or cumin chai latte frappés or whatever. Let someone else deal with the complaints that the free WiFi is too slow. Just get one of those industrial-strength Bunn coffee makers and a few pounds of sweaty coffee; call it a day.

DOWNSIZING

Large executive offices often foster resentment.

Employees don't get why the people who actually serve customers sit in crowded cube farms while the people who sit in meetings *talking about* the people who serve customers work in offices the size of a Wall Street ego.

You can go a long way towards building employee goodwill by downsizing your executive team's offices. Better yet, why not ask the executives to share office space? Given the twelve weeks' vacation and remote-work options available to them, there's a good chance that "sharing office space" will really just mean taking turns. As usual, keep that part to yourself.

Word will spread fast that you are building an egalitarian organization where everyone is valued, where even the big wigs are willing to relinquish something for the common good. But keep the floor security; you'll need it when the annual proxy statement comes out highlighting pay differentials.

Better Company Food

Employees demand a lot of their company cafeterias.

More than likely, your food service manager receives tons of requests. Actually, *more than* more than likely, they get more complaints than your HR department. They also receive direct threats—which is almost bound to happen when people get *hangry* and they want to shout at someone that seems responsible.

Here are some of the requests, complaints, and threats you might hear passed along through your food service:

- **Not enough (or too many) healthy food options**—if you don't have a fully stocked salad bar and plenty of paleo options, you're going to get an earful about it. At the same time, you don't want to make it too healthy or omit the junk food; what are you, a fascist?

- **Not enough bread-and-cheese options**—no matter how many dieticians you have giving health lectures, employees will still demand pizza and quesadillas. But, again, don't forget the salad bar; they still want to look at the green space.

- **Calls for cafeteria staff terminations**—because a salad bar worker who couldn't stock hearts of palm clearly doesn't deserve this job anymore.

Don't forget that you're also charged with serving foods that accommodate all special diets (such as the Blood Type Diet, Cabbage Soup Diet, and the Charcoal Cleanse), staffing a diverse and personable cafeteria team whose members *never* have a bad day (ever), and committing to only using produce grown with love.

Good luck with that.

Flexible Work

For the last couple of decades, employees have been challenging the parameters of traditional office work.

They ask why their performance is still being measured by how long they sit at a desk, inside of a building, for eight-plus hours at a time—a choice that someone made in the good old days, before electricity and indoor toilets were common.

Employees are proposing **something ludicrous: they want to be measured by their results** and have the flexibility to work *whenever* and *wherever* they want. They want time to do other things in their lives besides sit in meetings and develop PowerPoint presentations.

You may be shocked to learn that many of them don't thrill at these daily opportunities.

Perhaps you are still a proponent of "face time." *It's less about trusting people,* you say; it's more that you just don't know what the hell all of these people *do* every day. Seeing them at a desk looking busy scratches your alpha-boss itch, even when you walk past and spot them shopping on Amazon.

But with all of these younger people around—the Gen Xs and Ys and Zs and so forth—you need to become a more modern, more agile organization. This means:

- **People don't have to come in to the office to work.** You need to train the company leaders to lead virtually and challenge them to find creative ways to establish teamwork among people who don't see each other often.

- **Performance management changes.** You will need to establish clear, measurable, and purposeful goals for each employee's work so that each person understands what success looks like and what activities are needed to improve their personal performance.

- **Technology needs will increase.** More people will have need of digital tools such as teleconferencing, and so you will need to invest in new technology for connecting all of your people.

- **A change management initiative is required.** You will need a team of change agents to help people transition through the emotions this shift will bring.

Fuck it. Way too much trouble. *Vive le face time!*

Corporate Social Responsibility (CSR)

The new generation of workers has a lot of do-gooders. Not only do these people want their work to make a difference, but they also want *their employers* to give back to *their* communities. This has led to the popularity of CSR programs, which is where companies figure out how to spin a few ill-attended (or mandatory) volunteer activities into an inspirational 52-page report, complete with picture-perfect stock photos.

If you need ideas on padding a thin CSR report, consider the ideas on the following page:

1. **Decrease your electricity usage.** Employees will sweat when the air conditioning is turned off in August, but they'll be happy for it because they care. You'll be happier, too, when you hear how much you saved on overhead that month. It's a good thing that executives can work from home, am I right?

2. **Increase the diversity in your supply chain.** Don't just give business to men who like to chat over golf. Consider people who play tennis as well.

3. **Provide a paid day off for volunteering.** The executive team can make up lost productivity with one or two urgent weekend work requests. *Easy.*

Remember to consistently measure happiness with monthly surveys so that you can adjust and accommodate for employees—or just tell the unhappy ones to go whine to their life coaches.

CHAPTER 4
BUILD 'I'M SO BUSY' STREET CRED

A new authority in organizational development has appeared, and it's called *neuroscience*.

Neuroscience is the study of the nervous system, which until recently had been relegated to the field of biology. But some genius figured out there was big money to be made by introducing a discipline about nervousness to workplaces full of nervous people.

The neuroscience gurus will tell you that *status* is a fundamental human need. It seems we are always comparing ourselves to others to see how we stack up. We want to have the biggest office, the better title, and the closest parking space.

While these are certainly important markers of status, there is another badge of honor in corporate America that should not be overlooked:

Who's the *busiest* person in the place?

No matter how much people plead for work/life balance, what people really want is to be able to tell everyone just how *busy* they are. No matter the question posed to them, the reply will always be some twist on "I'm *sooooo* busy."

YOU: How have you been, Michelle?

MICHELLE: Busy!

YOU: Did you take a vacation this past summer?

MICHELLE: Yes, but I had to check my email every couple of hours because it's been *soooo* busy at work.

YOU: We've been lucky this winter with the weather being so warm.

MICHELLE: I guess, but my *crazy* busy schedule kept me indoors, so I haven't really noticed.

There are several leadership techniques available to help you meet this basic human need and keep your employees very busy, in word and action. This chapter outlines some tried-and-true methods.

Hold Lots of Pointless Meetings

Rest assured: when you start adding more and more meetings, your team members are going to complain, and loudly. They will say, "we are becoming a meeting culture," that "we have meetings to plan meetings," or that "we've got to do something about all the meetings around here."

But read between the lines for their "status" needs, and you will observe their swell of pride when they say they're quadruple-booked at 10 a.m.

There are plenty of meeting types from which to choose, all of which have the intended effect of instantly cluttering calendars:

Team meetings—Weekly *kumbayas* to build intimacy between people whose only connection is that they have the same idiot for a leader.

Department meetings—Create inclusiveness by allowing more people to hear the same thing that the senior team heard but couldn't be bothered to share in a single two-minute email.

One-on-one meetings (no, not the kind from a George Michael song)—Often the more productive meetings, but alas, the first ones to be canceled to make room for other meetings.

Engagement meetings—No one is sure why the first-ever engagement meeting was held, but the reason is probably exactly what this chapter is about: helping people feel better about themselves by making them arbitrarily busy.

Offsite planning meetings—Designed to force emotional bonding between people who don't like each other and to develop plans that two focused people could have done in an hour without leaving the office.

In addition to creating a high volume of meetings, there are a couple easy methods for making sure your meetings are wildly ineffective, all but guaranteeing you will need to hold another meeting to complete the tasks you didn't finish at the first one.

- **Invite way too many people.** This will guarantee that the meeting starts late and that nothing will be accomplished. If you haven't violated the room's fire code, you haven't done your job.

- **Leverage conference calls.** You can kill 30 minutes of an hour-long meeting simply by repeating everything you've discussed every time someone joins the call late.

Encourage Emails

Another surefire way to keep people busy is with email. Some have claimed that email will soon go the way of the dinosaur and will be replaced with a newer and more streamlined set of communication methods. Not to worry—employees secretly love email. Colleagues can't *wait* to tell each other how many emails they've received in a day, even if three-quarters of those emails are junk that they ignore.

In one recent study, workers noted that they spent more than six hours per day on email. Your team can do better than this. Mandate to the organization that, in an effort to create a more collaborative environment, employees will be penalized for not Replying to All on any business-related email. Everyone should be in the know about everything!

Create Cross-Functional Teams (CFTs) for Literally Everything

Cross-functional teams will keep even your star players overwhelmed for months. The beauty of these interdisciplinary efforts is that you **can justify creating them for just about any business challenge.**

CFTs (because you need an acronym for everything) consume an inordinate amount of time because they (1) require lots of meetings, (2) generate lots of emails, and (3) are typically created to solve intractable problems, problems that have existed for years and—if we're being honest—aren't likely to be solved by the CFT.

In even the worst cases, a single project or problem can tie people up for at least 18 months!

Examples of easy cross-functional opportunities are:

- Motivating employees to flush the toilets. The signs don't work.

- Developing an education campaign on the 15 bins in the cafeteria for recycling (paper, glass, plastic, cardboard, uranium, etc.), composting (banana peels, leftover vegetables, vegan poop), evil landfill trash, and anything else for hauling to the new chicken coop out back.

- Creating a notification system that immediately identifies any customers who have switched to a competitor so they can be targeted for daily email blasts. If you can't win them back, at least punish them for leaving.

Watch your employees feign anger as they gleefully talk up their heavy workloads. Remember: the anger only counts if they're not happy being busy—and of course they love being busy. Their reputations depend on it!

5 CHAPTER
DAZZLE WITH DECKS AND BUZZWORDS

As a leader rises through the ranks, he or she must be able to demonstrate a keen understanding of the business landscape.

Being strategic creates clear vision for the company—and inspires followers who believe that you can see into the future to guide the company successfully.

Leverage your inner Yoda, you must.

There is no time to lose, because no matter your other leadership gifts, you will be judged very harshly if you can't be described as "strategic."

Perhaps you are in a state of panic because your leadership strengths are in other areas, like . . .

Execution: a skill that was respected when you were a lowly front line supervisor, but proves a burden and a curse (it means you can do stuff, and that's not a good expectation to set as a supervisor).

Command-and-control leadership: You may have accomplished a lot with planning, directing, and scaring the bejesus out of your employees, but this leadership style is not considered to be "empowering." (See Chapter 1 on Culture for more about empowerment).

Creativity: If the company wanted a brainstorming, ideating nutcase as a leader, they likely would have promoted someone in the Training department.

Fortunately, there are a couple easy fixes to mask any gaps in this area and prove you have the strategic vision that every stakeholder is expecting you to have.

Dazzle with Buzzwords

Every couple of years, a set of new industry words emerges and takes the business world by storm.

You will command the respect of your employees, partners, and board members by peppering your conversations and presentations with as many such buzzwords as you can.

I've given some sample buzzwords below:

Consumer Experience: The days of talking about customer "service" have passed. "Service" gave way to "experience" several years ago and if this is news to you, you need more help than this book can provide. Declaring that your company will be creating a superior "consumer experience" will make you sound contemporary. And there are plenty of other experiences that need to be created, too—like the "employee experience," the "partner experience," and the "desktop dining experience." The world is your oyster.

Big Data: This is about data that is big, not small. That's about all you need to know to catch up to speed, because no one except your tech teams know what the hell this means.

Thought Leadership: The world of thoughts has always been in need of a strong leader, and that leader can be you. Action is overrated anyway. Being a thought leader will earn you many conference speaking engagements and a place in the Thought Leader Hall of Fame, complete with a trophy shaped like a brain. Even if you can't lead the thoughts of others, you can still be a thought leader for yourself just by, you know, thinking.

Design Thinking: Try connecting this to other buzzwords to form a powerful statement that shows your command of the business world:

"Through *design thinking,* we will gain insights that will enable us to transform the *consumer experience* and position ourselves as the industry's *thought leader* and *game-changer*."

Voilà! You're now a genius. That wasn't so hard, was it? Notice that I didn't have to tell you what *design thinking* is—which is convenient, because I don't know. With some practice, you'll get good at this too.

Deck the Halls

You don't want to hear this, trust me, but I have to tell you: at this point in your career, as a senior exec, your MBA is not nearly as valuable as your PowerPoint skills.

Most of your days will be spent developing, changing, or presenting a PowerPoint deck, and trying to sound happy about doing it when you'd prefer to be doing real work. (Well, you know, not *real* work, but something other than PowerPoint.)

Strategy and PowerPoint are a marriage made in heaven. You can't have a strategy without a PowerPoint presentation, although a good PowerPoint can *be* the strategy in a pinch.

Create effective PowerPoint decks by:

- **Spending an inordinate amount of time scrutinizing each word in a 50-page deck.** Gather your entire direct-report team around the table so they can chime in with word suggestions. It will come together beautifully by version 45, variant B. As a bonus, you will have succeeded in keeping everyone super-busy, too (for more on busyness, see Chapter 4).

- **Load your slides with lots of words.** Use small font to convey sensitive information. This is also a good *gotcha* tactic when one of your team members says she didn't know about a process change, for example. "It's Bullet 12 on Slide 56, Amy," you respond disdainfully. You'll have license to make fun of her reading comprehension for the next six weeks.

- **Unleash your inner artist.** Engage in deep creative discussions about whether you should depict the "industry landscape" with a stock photo of an English garden or a watercolor of desert wildflowers. Spend plenty of time making this decision; it's important that you don't pick the wrong one.

CHAPTER 6
RE-ORG SMORGASBORD

It's guaranteed that, during your tenure, you will lead *at least* one major restructuring of your organization.

I'm here to help you make the most of it.

It's unclear why so many executives feel compelled to overhaul their workplaces only minutes after arriving there—I can only guess it's like buying a new house and then finding you can't *possibly* live in it until the kitchen cabinets are replaced, the rooms get a fresh coat of paint, and the bathrooms all get double sinks.

You need to make the place your own, you know.

Of course, the *official* reasons for doing so are made clear to everyone: reduced costs, improved decision-making, and increased productivity. It's the "unofficial" reasons that represent your biggest opportunity.

A *re-org*, as it's fondly called, can be just what the doctor ordered when you need to:

- Demonstrate innovation but you're out of good ideas
- Keep people very busy and distract them from noticing your screw-ups
- "Relocate" your naysayers

Depending on what you most want to achieve—and the insecurities you most want to mask—there are a number of ways to approach this task with style.

Brand It

All initiatives must be well-branded, and the same is true of a re-org. (For more on branding itself, refer to the next chapter.) Fortunately, there are plenty of semantic options when it comes to constructing just the right identity for your personal vendetta (*ahem*, your re-org):

Transformation—a positive spin, since the term connotes a rebirth for you (even if it sometimes means other people's careers die in the process)

Streamlining—instills the most fear, since it implies that not everyone is going to have a chair when the music stops

Creating synergies—leverages jargon no one understands to convince people there must be some higher reasoning behind these decisions

Combining ingredients—evokes warm, homey feelings of Grandma, the kitchen, and warm apple pie (yet conveniently *doesn't* remind people that you have to break eggs to bake, well, nearly anything)

Plan Your Approach

It's your choice. You can do this thing quickly or drag it out, nice and slow. Your options boil down to:

1. **Stringing them along.** Announcing an upcoming re-org will automatically paralyze people with fear. If you are suffering from a fear of failure yourself, instilling a bit of fear into others is, well, just paying it forward. One way to torture your challengers is to create an eternally lengthy planning process that pushes people to their mental limits while they wait to learn whether they still have a job or (worse) if they will be reporting to a peer!

2. **Shock and awe.** This military-style tactic can be an effective corporate trick for showing strength and power. Planning and executing a re-org quickly will show others that you are decisive, a force to be reckoned with. Drones can also be utilized to eavesdrop on meetings where subordinates are most certainly planning a corporate coup. (It's wise to be a little paranoid.)

Creatively Combine

When it comes to reorganizing, the notion of centralizing or decentralizing functions is so passé. A creative third option, however, has been about as easy to find as another species that can ride horses while eating cake.

Rest easy—we've developed several ideas that will showcase just how creative and innovative a leader you are when it comes to stirring things up. Here is some out-of-the-box thinking for your next re-alignment:

- **Combine Marketing with Accounting.** This is one way to further your stated objective of "constructive conflict." Note that it may take some time to get to the *constructive* part of "constructive conflict."

- **Integrate IT and HR.** You will create camaraderie by combining the two-most hated departments in the company. At least they have this in common, right?

- **Create rotations between Sales and Service** so the Sales team can finally learn what it's like to have to make good on your promises.

Last but not least, a re-org is also an opportunity to build your team and determine who's "in" and who's "out." Sure, ability matters, but what's more important is who you can tolerate being around for the multitude of meetings, off-sites, retreats, and whatever else you need to do to prove you're *all about* collaboration.

Rinse and Repeat

The great thing about re-orgs is that you can always find a good reason to repeat the cycle—and practice makes perfect. Once you get the hang of it, you'll find it's as simple as taking out the email announcement from the last re-org and just changing up the names.

Employees often expect re-orgs to happen with some regularity, so no one will call you to task if you lead them over . . .

. . . and over . . .

. . . and over again.

"It's not what you know.
It's what you can prove."

— *Denzel Washington* as
Detective Alonzo Harris

Defend the Results

Some have claimed that most corporate restructurings do not produce the business results they are supposed to achieve. There may be a kernel of truth in this if, and only if, you are confining your definition of success to the narrow metric of financial performance.

But, as the supreme leader, you know better, and you know how to think BIGGER. A re-org isn't strictly about the money; you know that even the *hint* of one moves the needle more on busyness, productivity and motivation than anything else in your bag of tricks.

Once the news breaks, employees will be busier than ever talking with colleagues, speculating on the latest rumors, including which leaders are at risk for getting voted off the island and who they better start sucking up to, *pronto*.

These situations also prompt deep reflection as individuals contemplate how their talents will be used in the organization going forward, or whether they will have the luck of being supported in their "pursuit of outside opportunities."

The Water Cooler will be a very happening place indeed.

CHAPTER 7

BLOW UP THE BRAND

There will come a time in your career when you will be called upon to reinvigorate the brand.

Maybe sales have been declining, you've missed earnings forecasts the last three quarters, and the new member of the Board is pissed that your brand equity numbers are in the toilet.

You can count on your marketing team to get excited and propose several ideas, any of which will cost a fortune. Apparently, as they've told you, consumer research has revealed that your company is known as the "Corvette of the industry." That was cool in the seventies—not so much in this century.

There is only one way to go . . .

Redefining the Brand

Of course, this task will require the time and talents of multiple high-end consultants in New York to:

- **Research your competitors' color wheels.** These ivy-league MBAs will identify the precise color hue that is currently dominating your industry so you can adjust your own and then claim a differentiated value proposition. If your competitors have chocolate brown brand colors, make a strategic pivot to Brown Sugar or Mississippi Mud Pie (or the color of a river you'd never swim in).

- **Conduct thousands of focus groups.** In order to prove your company is focused on the consumer experience, the consultants will talk to hundreds of people to determine whether they prefer the squiggly line coming out of the top or the bottom part of the logo. These things matter greatly to people when they're making a purchase.

- **Leverage your knowledge of abnormal personality traits to create customer profiles.** Effective marketing is about knowing the characteristics and neuroses of people in the market for your product so you can appeal to them personally.

  For example, there is the "Daphne" persona, the obsessively-organized wedding planner who needs you to provide all information in a bulleted list.

  And there is "Grant," the environmentalist who wants all mailed communications printed on recycled bark.

- **Create reams of PowerPoint presentations.** Consultants will create multiple decks with terminology that no one understands like Brand Identity, Brand Voice, Brand Promise, Brand Hierarchy, and Brand Genealogy Tree. Everyone will want to know the heritage of the brand, how each word came about, and if any of these words were conceived out of wedlock.

When they've finished their work, cherish the heft of the binder they give you and move your hand slowly over the embossed cover. Take a good, long look at what you've received for those investment dollars, because once you put it down, you will never look at it again.

Launching the Brand

You now have everything you need to move forward with the brand re-launch. At this point, you need to go *big*.

No doubt some nerves tingle when you hear this, since it has already cost millions of dollars to create the new brand (and its fancy PowerPoints), but this next step is essential for consumer and employee engagement. The rollout plan involves a few simple elements:

The tear-jerker video. There is nothing like an over-the-top emotional video to welcome a new corporate brand. If people don't cry, you have failed. Take a cue from the ASPCA commercials with Sarah McLachlan; they *nailed* it.

The launch party. Preferably in an auditorium with balloons coming down from the ceiling and gifts for employees such as oversized t-shirts and more of those branded ballpoint pens for their treasured corporate giveaway collection.

New print and TV commercials. Because the old ones you have already paid to develop are now "off-brand."

A new company spokesperson. If you can't get Ryan Gosling, try Jerry Springer (or OJ Simpson, if you feel like living dangerously).

A major PR campaign. You will need to sponsor events that showcase your company's new brand. If budget is an issue, less expensive events worth considering include the Waco Hot Dog Eating Contest and the Retired Cowboys Violin Concerto.

A new brand will generate excitement among your employees. No one except the marketing team will understand exactly what you mean by Brand Identity, but all will cheer the new logo and fantasize happily about the hours of fun they will have placing it on PowerPoint templates and email signatures.

CHAPTER 8
VOTE FOR THE FINAL CHAPTER

What did I miss?
I'd love your help to write the last chapter(s).

Please **visit my professional Facebook page (Elizabeth H. George)** or
email me at ehgeorge@truesouthbook.com

. . . to pass along your suggestions, and to **sign up for my mailing list** to be notified about future publications.

And if you enjoyed the book, feel free to tell your friends, family, colleagues, and even your boss about it.

I will write subsequent chapters based on reader feedback, and the new material will appear in the next version of the book!

AUTHOR'S
ACKNOWLEDGEMENTS

First, I'd like to thank the Academy.
Oh wait—wrong speech.

All kidding aside, I would like to thank several people who contributed to making this book a reality. My thanks go to Doug Campau, Ellen Nason, Jenn Forst, and Lisa Hunt for their invaluable feedback, and to Kevin Williamson of Red Letter Publishing for helping bring out the best in this work. My appreciation also goes to Simon Goodway for his wonderful illustrations. Finally, I'm eternally grateful to my husband, Peyman Attari, for reading *True South* at least a thousand times and providing helpful comments each time.

I also want to acknowledge two other writers whose books proudly sit on my shelves: Elizabeth George, the great mystery novelist, and Bill George, the leadership guru whose wonderful book *True North* inspired this title. I haven't met either of them, but I've long respected their work (and am not-so-secretly hoping our shared names will bump my book sales a little bit).

Lastly, thank you to all the people out there who take risks and follow their own crazy paths. You inspire me.

Elizabeth H. George is a recovering corporate professional who still enjoys throwing jargon around from time to time.

Elizabeth lives in Louisville, Kentucky.

www.ingramcontent.com/pod-product-compliance
Lightning Source LLC
Chambersburg PA
CBHW050602300426
44112CB00013B/2040